Ray Vander Laan

LIVING IN THE MASTER'S PLAN

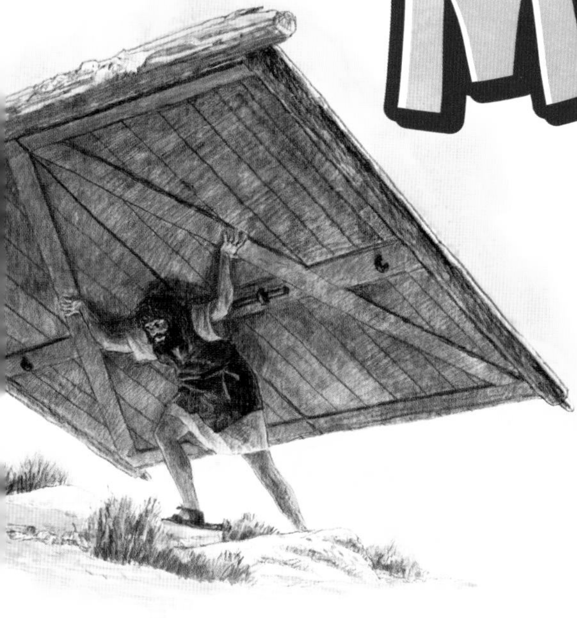

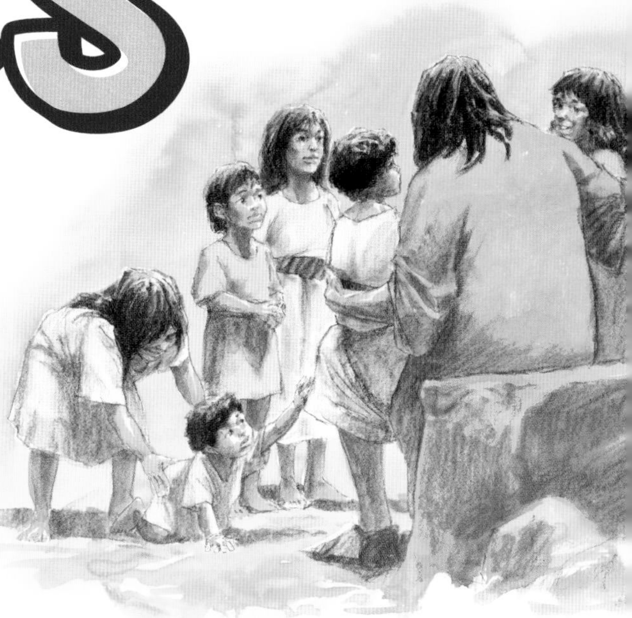

30 FAMILY DEVOTIONS

Tyndale House Publishers, Inc.
Carol Stream, Illinois

Living in the Master's Plan

Editor: Haley Mader
Cover design by Josh Lewis

For information about special discounts for bulk purchases, please contact Tyndale House Publishers at csresponse@tyndale.com, or call 1-800-323-9400.

ISBN 978-1-5899-7707-5

Printed in China

26 25 24 23 22 21 20
7 6 5 4 3 2 1

For more than 25 years, Focus on the Family has been privileged to partner with Ray Vander Laan in developing *That the World May Know*. Ray's timeless teaching brings God's Word to life in amazing and profound ways. His understanding of Scripture, coupled with his humility and passionate walk with Christ, have impacted countless people for nearly three decades.

Now, Focus is honored to present Ray's teaching in a format that is designed specifically for you to share with your children and grandchildren. *Living in the Master's Plan* is a beautifully illustrated series of 30 devotions for you to enjoy around the dinner table, in morning devotions, with bedtime prayers, or at any time you set aside to draw your family into a deeper walk with Christ.

We pray that you are deeply blessed by this unique devotional book. May it help you and your family walk more closely in the footsteps of our Master.

Jim Daly
President
Focus on the Family

1 Standing Stones

A long time ago, the people of ancient Israel set up "standing stones" in certain places that were special to them. They would take large stones, some more than twenty feet tall, and work together to stand them up in holes they had dug in the ground. Why would they make the time to do that?

> "On that day Joshua made a covenant for the people, and there at Shechem he reaffirmed for them decrees and laws. And Joshua recorded these things in the Book of the Law of God. Then he took a large stone and set it up there under the oak near the holy place of the Lord."
>
> *Joshua 24:25-26*

Well, when something important happened, such as a battle, a treaty, or a miracle, the Israelites would stand the stones in the ground to be a symbol to other people around them that God had done something amazing for His people. People would see the stones and say, "Wow, your God must be something else."

Did you know you are a "standing stone" for God? He has done amazing things in your life, and He wants you to tell others what He's done. When you tell your story, you are influencing people around you for the Lord.

Maybe He saved your life during an accident. Maybe He helped you keep your temper when you were really angry at someone. It doesn't matter if it is big or small. What matters is that God did something in your life, and we are told to share what He has done with the people around us.

So who can you tell? Do you have friends at school or even a teacher you can share your story with? What about your teammates on a sports team? How about your cousin? It doesn't matter how old you are, God wants to use you to tell others about what He's done in your life so He can do the same for them.

Let's Talk About It

What are two things God has done in your life that you could tell others about?

Did You Know?

Standing stones can be huge! They can weigh more than 25 tons each, can stand 20 feet tall, and are sunk 20 feet into the earth.

2 Crossing the Jordan

The Jordan River in Israel isn't very big. But when it floods, the river grows much wider, and the water rushes downstream at top speed. The white, churning water splashes violently over the rocks.

The Israelites were supposed to cross this flooding river to get to the Promised Land, the place God was giving to them. But how could they cross it without drowning? The raging river blocked them—it was a pretty big barrier.

The Canaanites on the other side of the river believed that a false god, Baal, was in charge of the Jordan River. But the Israelites knew their God was the God of everything, even the frightening river.

God told the Israelite priests to get their feet wet—to step into the water. Once they did that, God parted the river so all the Israelites could cross it. Those priests stepped into that river with total faith in the God they believed. And the whole community crossed over into the land God gave them. The priests' choice made a difference!

Your choices make a difference, too. When have you "got your feet wet" for God? Have you made choices to step out in faith, even if there was a scary barrier? Have you asked a neighbor kid to go with you to a church event or talked about Jesus to someone at school? Did you decide to sing in the choir at church, even if you were nervous about it?

Remember, God is the God of everything. He will go before you and can get you across any barrier as you step out in faith for Him.

> "The Lord himself goes before you and will be with you; he will never leave you nor forsake you. Do not be afraid; do not be discouraged."
>
> *Deuteronomy 31:8*

Let's Talk About It

How does God want you to step out in faith for Him?

If you don't know, pray and ask God about it. Then listen for an answer.

Did You Know?

The Jordan River flows for 200 miles from Mount Hermon to the Dead Sea.

Did You Know?

The Jordan River is one of the fastest-flowing rivers in the world for its size.

3 The Battle of Jericho

After the Israelites entered the Promised Land, God wanted them to have the city of Jericho. So God gave the Israelites specific instructions to march around the city thirteen times and blow their trumpets when He told them to. If they obeyed God and did things His way, the Israelites would win this first battle in the Promised Land.

If you were there, you would have seen that the walls around Jericho were incredibly high, as tall as a four-story building in a modern city!

Marching around those walls probably didn't seem like what an army should do, but the Israelites obeyed God and followed His orders. They knew the battle belonged to God, not them. God was in charge, and He knew how to fight and win. The Israelites just had to follow His commands.

You might have a battle before you, too. Maybe someone at school wants you to help her cheat on a test, or is showing you stuff on his phone that you know is wrong for you to see, or is saying lies about someone. How do you fight this battle? You do what's right, what God has commanded you to do. You don't lie, you don't look at evil things, you stand for the truth, and you obey your parents. All you have to do is follow God's commands. Then He will fight the battle for you!

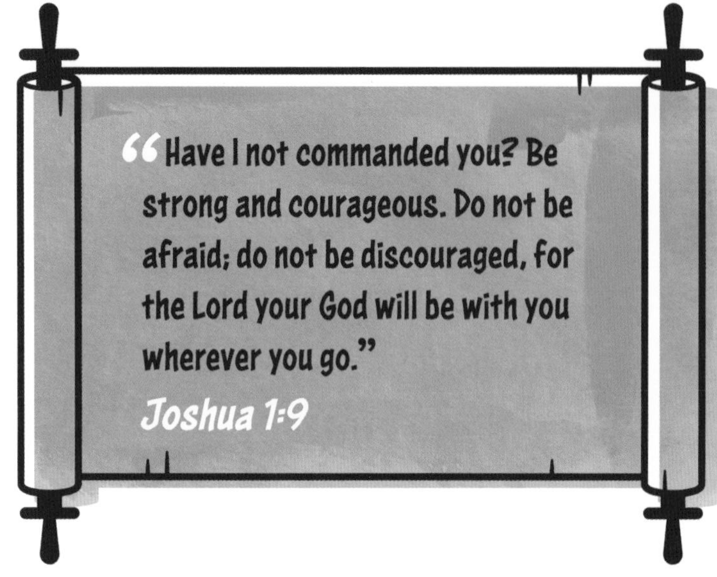

Let's Talk About It

What battle or problem do you have and are wondering what to do?

Ask God to help you follow His commands and to fight the battle for you. Talk to your parents about it, too.

Did You Know?

Jericho was the first city captured by the Israelites after wandering in the desert for 40 years.

4 Samson and the Philistines

After the Israelites entered the Promised Land, they were supposed to conquer the pagan people there. But the Tribe of Dan never did drive out the Philistines, and this caused plenty of problems.

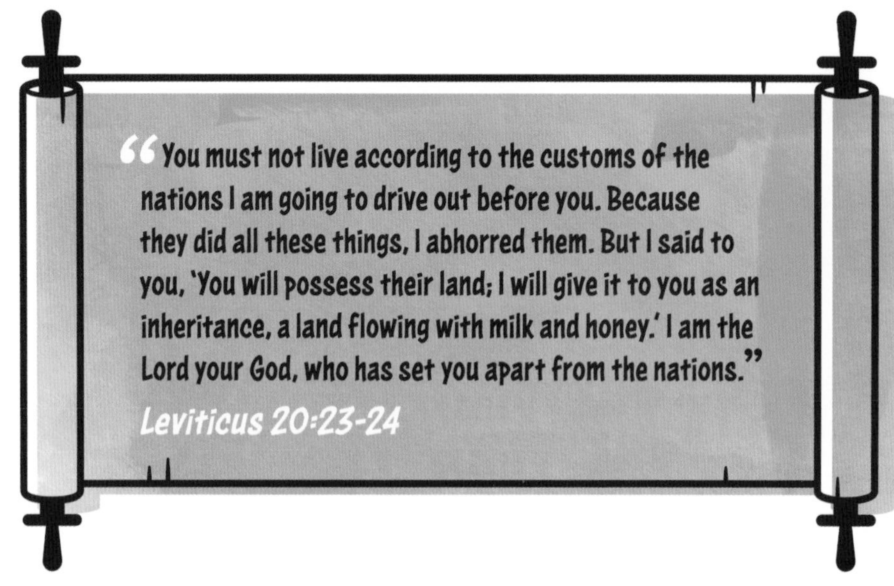

The Philistines were wicked and worshipped things that God says are evil. God wanted His people to be set apart, to be different from the Philistines and the way they lived. To remind them of that, He told Samson’s parents to make their son a Nazirite. As a Nazirite, Samson could not cut his hair, drink wine, or eat meat. Samson was an example of how different the Israelites were supposed to be from the Philistines. He was supposed to remind God’s people to do things God’s way, not the Philistine way.

When Samson followed God’s ways, he was strong and powerful. He even carried a city’s gate for forty-five miles! But when he started hanging out with the Philistines, doing things their way and letting them cut his hair, he lost all his strength and power.

Which kind of Samson are you? The one who was set apart or the one who hung out with the wrong crowd? Are you hanging out with the things God values? Or are you watching certain video games or other things that God doesn’t like? If you want to be strong for God, you’ll need to be “set apart,” different from the people who don’t know God.

Let’s Talk About It

What makes you different from others who don’t know God? Are you “set apart”?

Is there something you need to change so you can be set apart?

Did You Know?

Samson made a vow to never cut his hair or beard, to abstain from any grape product, and to avoid contact with anything dead.

Did You Know?

He carried the gate 45 miles on his shoulders.

5 David and Goliath

The Philistines were fighting the Israelites, and the Israelites were scared. The Philistines had a nine-foot-tall giant named Goliath to fight for them.

The Israelites had no one courageous enough to face this giant. No one, that is, until a shepherd boy named David showed up. He was probably around your age—about ten or twelve years old.

When David heard Goliath making fun of the Israelites' God, he knew he had to do something! David didn't have a sword or spear, but he had great faith in God. He wanted the whole world to know that there "is a God in Israel" and that He is a powerful God! So God used David's gift of throwing stones with a slingshot to topple the giant.

David was successful because he wasn't fighting for himself—he was fighting so everyone would know about God. And he was successful because he wasn't trying to be like anyone else. He didn't try to use the soldier's armor that didn't fit him. He simply used the gifts and skills God had given him to do the fighting.

Remember, God has given you special talents, too. You don't need to be like anyone else to do good things for God. You just have to use the gifts God gave you and be yourself! Maybe you're good at encouraging other people and being kind. Maybe you're good at math or soccer, or at helping in the kitchen or taking care of animals.

To make a difference in the world, you don't have to be anything other than what God has created you to be!

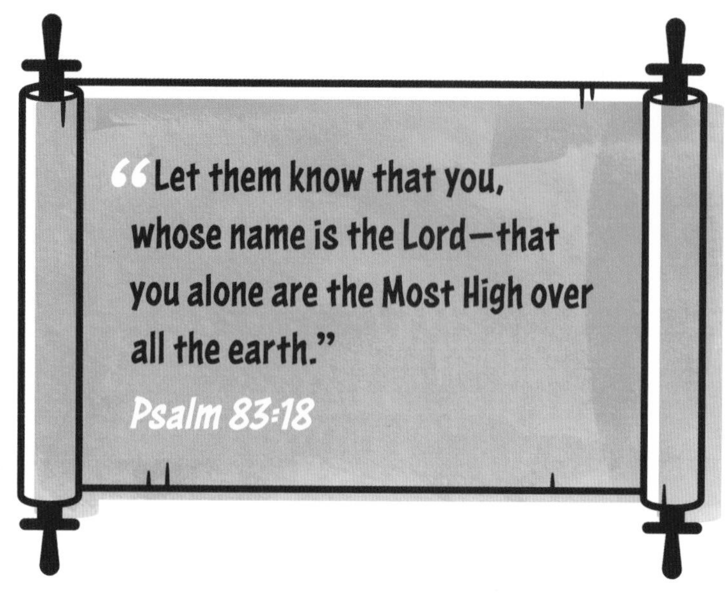

Let's Talk About It

Which of your talents might God want to use today?

Did You Know?

David fought Goliath in the Valley in the Shephelah between the coastal plain and the Judea Mountains.

6

Elijah

Elijah was a prophet, and God gave him a special job to do. He called Elijah to bring the Israelites back to God's ways. In Elijah's time, the Israelites, and even their king, were worshiping Baal, the false god of the Canaanite people. Baal was popular among the people, probably because he wasn't real and believing in this false god allowed them to do evil things.

To bring the Israelites back to God, Elijah gathered the people and the 450 prophets of Baal and the 400 prophets of Asherah to Mount Carmel. Then he challenged them, asking the prophets to show Baal's power by having their god burn the bull sacrificed on the altar there. The Baal prophets prayed to their god, but nothing happened.

When Elijah asked the one true God to burn the sacrifice, God immediately sent fire to burn it. It was an amazing display of power, and the Israelites cried out, "Yahweh, he is God!"

Because Elijah had a relationship with God, he didn't go along with the popular crowd of people who had forgotten about God. Elijah was able to do his job by reminding the Israelites about the real God.

Being popular doesn't make wrong actions right, even if a lot of people seem to be doing those things. So if some popular kids are bullying a kid with a disability, it's still wrong. We bring glory to God by doing the right things, not the popular things. If you stay in relationship with God, He will give you power to do the right things, just as He did for Elijah.

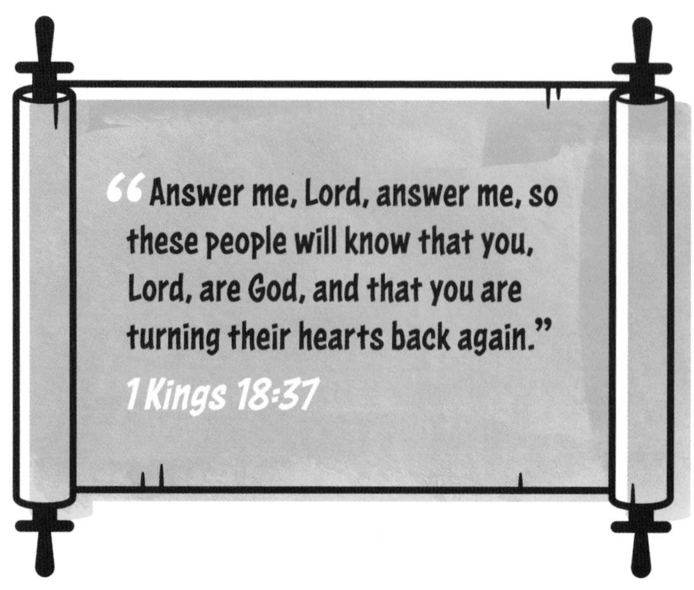

Let's Talk About It

How important is it for you to be popular?

Do you know of any popular things that aren't right according to God?

Did You Know?

Elijah's name literally means "Yahweh is God."

7 Hezekiah

Have you ever been around people who were doing the wrong thing? King Hezekiah was in that situation. He was the king of Judah during a time when most people chose to worship idols.

But Hezekiah destroyed the idols. He worshipped and obeyed God. Hezekiah persuaded the people to follow the one true God.

While Hezekiah was king, the king of Assyria attacked and conquered many cities near Jerusalem, where Hezekiah lived. The Assyrian king said to the people of Jerusalem, "What makes you think your God is going to protect you?"

> "Hezekiah trusted in the Lord, the God of Israel. There was no one like him among all the kings of Judah, either before him or after him. He held fast to the Lord and did not stop following him; he kept the commands the Lord had given Moses. And the Lord was with him; he was successful in whatever he undertook. He rebelled against the king of Assyria and did not serve him."
>
> 2 Kings 18:5-7

But Hezekiah had faith in God. He told the people that the king of Assyria only had human strength, but the people of Judah had the Lord to help them. Hezekiah built a tunnel to provide fresh water for his people in case the Assyrian king attacked. Hezekiah prayed and asked for God's help. God sent an angel to defeat the Assyrian army. The king went home in shame because he couldn't conquer Jerusalem.

God chose Hezekiah to be the king. He was just the right person, and he became king at just the right time so that he could serve God. King Hezekiah trusted God, but he also did everything he could to stand up to the king of Assyria.

The Bible tells us that our wise God has placed all of us at just the right time and at just the right place so we can serve Him. That means God has a plan for you and you have a job to do. God wants us to be prepared and ready to do what we can do, just like Hezekiah.

Let's Talk About It

What do you think God wants you to do today?

Did You Know?

Hezekiah was only 25 years old when he became king of Judah.

Did You Know?

The tunnel ranks as one of the engineering marvels of the ancient world.

8 The Shepherd

In Bible times, many people raised sheep. Sheep don't do a good job taking care of themselves. They need help finding water and food. They also need protection, because they don't have a good way to defend themselves from danger. Sheep need shepherds to guide them and protect them.

There is a special relationship between a shepherd and his sheep. The shepherd is always with his sheep. The shepherd leads them, and the sheep follow their shepherd. The sheep learn to recognize the shepherd's voice.

Sheep never need to worry about whether they will be hungry or thirsty. The shepherd finds green grass and good water for them each day. Sheep don't need to be scared of predators. They can sleep in peace at night because the shepherd is always on the lookout for wolves and other wild animals. The sheep trust the shepherd to take good care of them.

Sometimes a sheep will wander away and get lost. But a shepherd will search for the sheep until it is found. A good shepherd will even lay down his own life in order to protect his sheep.

The Bible says that we're like sheep and that Jesus is our shepherd. Jesus does all the things for us that a good shepherd does for his sheep. We can trust Jesus just as sheep trust their shepherd. Jesus provides for our needs each day. We can tell Him about our needs and know He hears us. Jesus tells us what is right and wrong. We can learn to recognize His voice. When we face difficult or scary things, Jesus guides us and protects us. But we must learn to listen and to follow Him, just as the sheep do their shepherd.

> "The Lord is my shepherd, I lack nothing. He makes me lie down in green pastures, he leads me beside quiet waters, he refreshes my soul. He guides me along the right paths for his name's sake."
>
> *Psalm 23:1-3*

Let's Talk About It

How has Jesus been a good shepherd to you?

What can you do to follow your Shepherd more closely?

Did You Know?

A shepherd's rod was used to guide and protect the sheep.

9 A King and a Baby

Who is more powerful, a king or a baby? The answer to this question might be different from what you think. King Herod, who was known as Herod the Great, was a powerful man. He was king for more than forty years, and he controlled more territory than almost any other king of the Jews. But he was a cruel king. He was quick to kill his enemies.

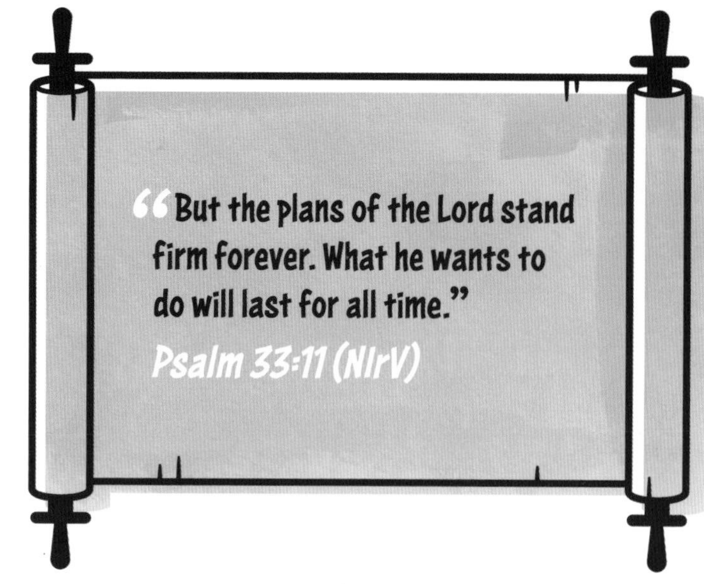

King Herod was famous for building huge fortress-palaces. One palace had a swimming pool that was twice as big as a modern-day Olympic pool. The pool was surrounded with beautiful gardens. When people saw Herod's magnificent buildings, they were reminded of just how powerful he was. That's just what King Herod wanted people to think.

During Herod's reign, a baby was born to a poor, ordinary family. He was born in a stable because His parents couldn't find a room in an inn. When this baby grew up, He didn't build any fortresses or palaces. In fact, sometimes He didn't even have a place to sleep in. He spent His time helping others, teaching them, and healing them. The baby's name was Jesus!

King Herod worked to bring glory to himself, but Jesus worked to serve others and bring glory to His heavenly Father. Herod seemed powerful, but Jesus is the One with real power. Jesus lived a simple life, but He has made a bigger change in the world than any king who has ever lived.

Herod may have been a king, but Jesus is King of the universe. Herod may have built fortresses, but the Bible says that God is our fortress. He is our place of safety!

Sometimes the bad people of the world seem to have all the power. It's easy to be scared. However, we can be courageous because our God is stronger than any evil or any ruler.

Let's Talk About It

How can knowing about God's power help you be courageous?

Did You Know?

Herod's palace contained pools and gardens.

Did You Know?

Herod's palace had walls rising more than 45 feet high.

10 The Essenes

The Essenes were a group of Jews who lived about the same time as Jesus. They loved God and wanted to live for Him.

The Essenes didn't want to be influenced by evil. They wanted to live pure and holy lives. They moved away from the cities and formed communities in the desert wilderness where they could devote themselves to God.

They thought it was important to live in fellowship with one another and to treat one another well. They shared all their belongings.

The Essenes wrote books about how to live for God. The Bible was very important to them. There were no printers or copy machines, so the Essenes copied the books of the Old Testament by hand on scrolls. They saved all their writings in clay jars that they put into caves so that the writings would be protected from the harsh environment of the desert.

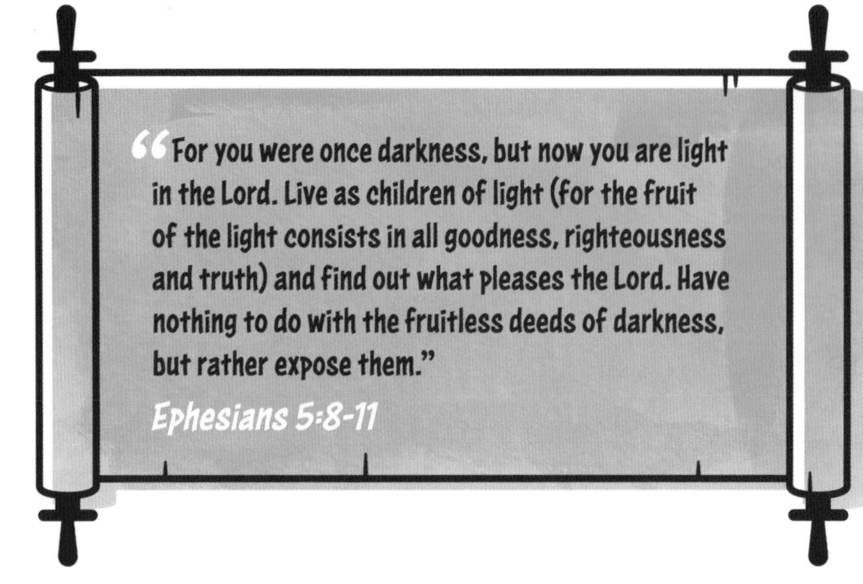

Much of what the Essenes did was very good. They truly wanted to worship God and honor Him with their lives. But they didn't understand how important it is to tell others about God. Instead, they kept all their knowledge about God to themselves out in the desert.

It can be difficult to live the way God wants us to live in a world where so many people do not know Him or live for Him. But how can others find out about God unless we tell them the good news?

When we live for God, we are like lights that shine in a dark world. We need to share the light with others.

Let's Talk About It

Who can you tell about Jesus?

Did You Know?

Archaeologists have found tables, benches, inkpots, and basins used by scribes.

Did You Know?

There are many similarities between the Essenes' ceremonial meal and the Last Supper.

11 The Rabbi

In Jesus' day, there was no such thing as church. Instead, those who believed in God went to synagogue to learn and to worship. The teacher at the synagogue was known as a rabbi.

The rabbi taught from the Torah, the first five books of the Old Testament. The scrolls of the Torah were very holy. They were kept in a special closet or cupboard. The people listened respectfully when the Torah was read. After the reading, the rabbi could make comments about what was read in order to teach the people about God.

Jesus was known as a rabbi. He taught in the synagogue. One day He read the verses to the right. It was important to Jesus to love and help people who were hurting. Jesus taught people how to find forgiveness for the wrong things they did. And Jesus taught people how to love one another and how to love God.

Every teacher needs students. A rabbi's students were called his disciples. It wasn't enough for a rabbi's disciples to learn from the rabbi. The disciples wanted more than anything else to be like their rabbi—to know what he knew and to do what he did. Jesus' disciples were no different. They wanted to be just like Jesus in every way.

Today, Jesus' followers are still called His disciples. If you are a Christian, you are a disciple! It's important for Jesus' disciples to learn about Him, but it's just as important to live like Jesus. Each day we can become more like Him in our thoughts and in our actions.

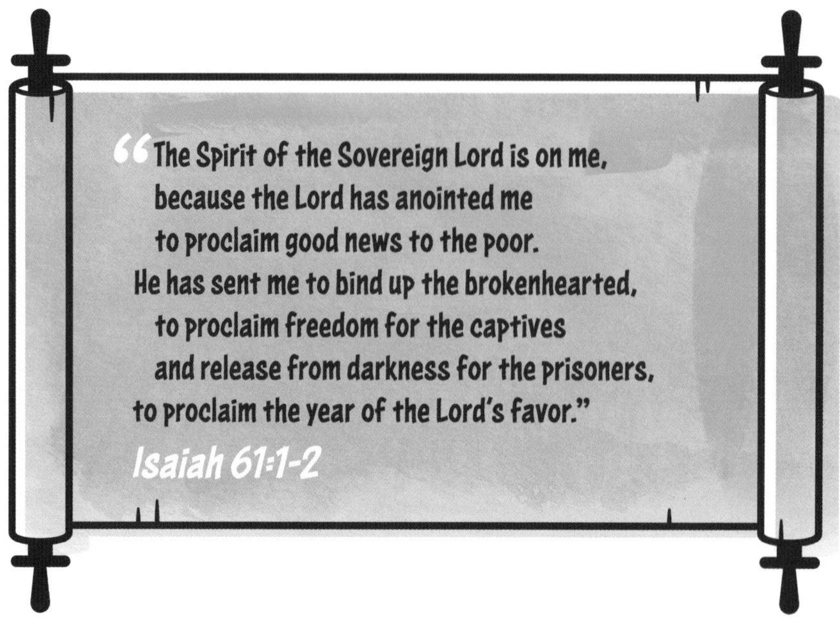

Let's Talk About It

What can you do today to become more like Jesus, your Rabbi?

Did You Know?

The Torah is the five books of Moses.

Did You Know?

A tallith, or Jewish prayer shawl, was worn by the rabbi.

12 The Theater

Sepphoris was a wealthy city on a hilltop. It could be seen for miles. Villas with mosaic floors lined its streets. King Herod owned a magnificent palace there, and Sepphoris' theater held more than 4,000 people.

The plays in this theater often mocked honorable and sacred things. Some even had R-rated tales. Actors in the theater painted their faces. The Greek word for an actor is *hypocrite*. Hypocrites were said to have two faces, their own and a painted one. They were called two-faced.

Three miles south of Sepphoris was another hill. On this hill was the town of Nazareth. That's where Jesus grew up. He knew what concerned farmers and what made the rich angry. He understood the problems of blind men and saw the pride of leaders. Knowing the people of His day helped Jesus talk to them.

Some of these people served God. Some didn't. Jesus wasn't scared of talking to believers and nonbelievers. He spoke to them about topics that were important to them. Jesus used word pictures and stories to teach people about their faith. The stories were called parables. Jesus told many parables. He told them about fishermen and kings. He told them about the wealthy and the poor. Jesus even used the word *hypocrite*, and everyone knew exactly what He meant.

There are many stories in our world today. What kind of stories do you listen to? What kind of stories do you tell? How do these stories help you share God's love with others?

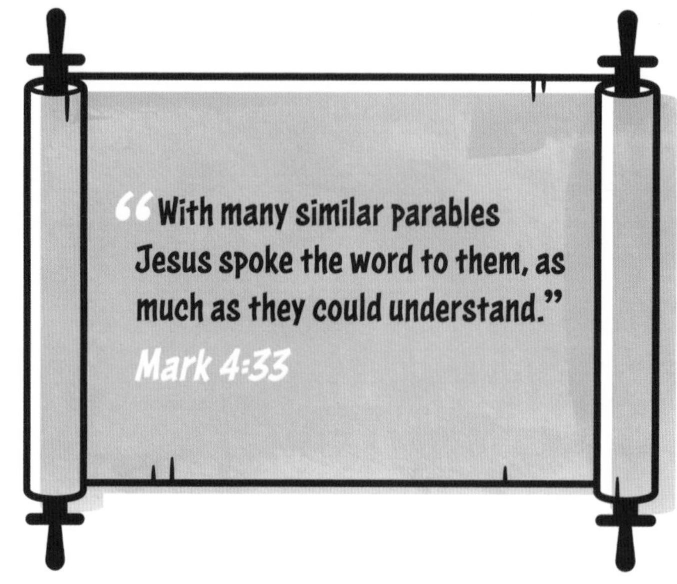

Let's Talk About It

What story has helped you understand God better?

How might this story help others?

Did You Know?

The Greek word for a "stage actor" was *hypocrite*.

Did You Know?

Plays often focused on false gods and goddesses.

13 The Crusades

Fort Belvoir stood on a hill overlooking the Jordan Valley. Fifty knights and 450 soldiers, along with their families and servants, lived there. They were Crusaders.

They'd come to kill anyone who didn't believe in their God. For almost 200 years, these knights and soldiers, and others like them, murdered Jewish, Muslim, and even Christian people in the Middle East.

These warriors thought they were serving God. They fought because their church leaders and kings told them to fight. But the Crusaders acted the opposite of how Jesus wanted His followers to behave. He didn't want them to hurt people they didn't understand. What they did was evil.

In Bible times, Jesus encountered evil wherever He went. Sometimes it came in the form of mean people who rejected what He said. Other times it showed up in those who were demon-possessed or hurt. Sometimes it even came through the words of His closest friends.

No matter where evil appeared, Jesus found a way to defeat it. He didn't use the weapons of the Crusaders. Instead, He used love, compassion, forgiveness, and self-sacrifice. Consider what might happen if you told people about God's message and fought evil the way Jesus did.

God doesn't want His people to treat strangers or neighbors poorly. Instead, Jesus wants you to be His hands and feet here on earth. He wants you to show others, even those who are unkind, how much He loves them. When you treat others well, you show them God's love and God's character.

Rely on Jesus. Follow His example and treat others well. His love conquers evil.

> "Follow God's example, therefore, as dearly loved children and walk in the way of love, just as Christ loved us and gave himself up for us as a fragrant offering and sacrifice to God."
>
> *Ephesians 5:1-2*

Let's Talk About It

Who is an unkind person in your life?

What can you do to show this person God's love?

Did You Know?

The Crusades formally ended in 1291.

14 En Gedi

God's people lived in the Judea wilderness for many years. This hot, dry land sapped their strength and made them weary. So God created places like En Gedi.

En Gedi is an amazing oasis. This desert spring isn't large, but water streams down its rocks and transforms the desert into a lush, beautiful land.

For centuries, travelers have stopped at En Gedi. This oasis soothed many parched throats, and people found rest there. In the same way, Jesus offers His children living water. He understands that we grow weary. So He has provided a way to refresh us. And He is willing to give us His living water every day of our lives. God is our En Gedi. Through Him, we find the courage to face another trip into our own hard situations.

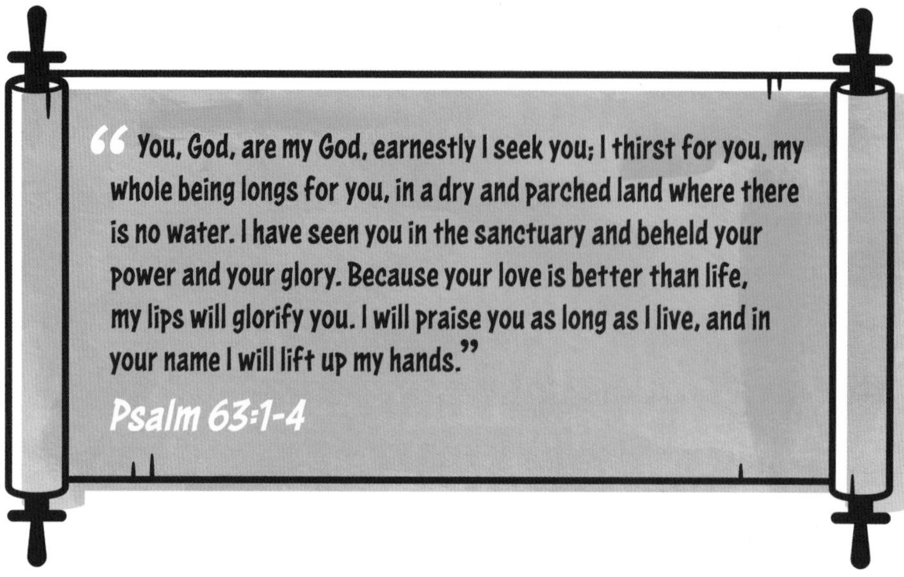

How do we drink this living water? Sometimes we drink it through reading God's Word, the Bible. Sometimes we get it when we pray to Him and listen for His voice. Sometimes other Christians encourage us to continue in our relationship with God. And sometimes it only takes worshiping God for us to feel renewed.

When we do these activities—Bible reading, prayer, fellowship, worship—we are drinking God's living water. How thirsty are you? Sometimes you may only take a sip, saying one small prayer. Other times you may worship and listen to God's Word with others at church, taking a large drink from the well.

God's living water is always available to you. When you are tired, drink deeply and regain your strength.

Let's Talk About It

How will you drink from God's living water today?

Did You Know?

David and his men hid from King Saul here.

15 The Disciples' Catch

Many people in Jesus' day lived on the shores of the Sea of Galilee and worked as fishermen. Some days they caught many fish. Other days they didn't catch anything. Sometimes they didn't even feel like trying to catch fish.

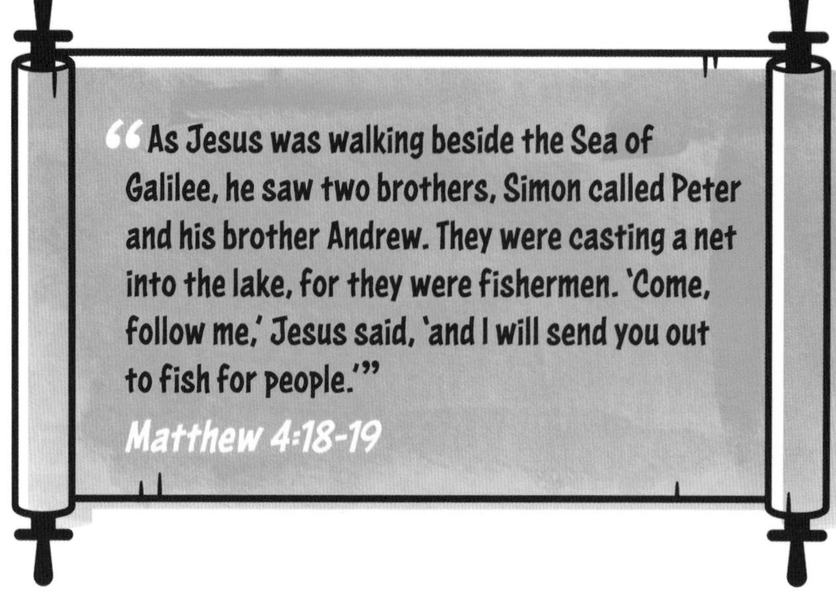

One day Jesus climbed into Simon Peter's boat. Peter had been fishing all night and hadn't caught anything. Jesus asked Peter to push the boat a little way into the sea. He wanted to speak to the crowd without being bumped.

After Jesus spoke, He told Peter to let down his nets. Peter didn't see the point but chose to do what Jesus asked. Peter caught so many fish that his nets almost broke. He had to call his fishing partners for help to get the catch to shore.

Jesus wasn't just about catching fish. He was finding disciples, those willing to try what He asked them to do. Many of these fishermen became God's fishers of men.

After Jesus rose from the dead, a similar story happened. Peter and other disciples went fishing. They fished all night but didn't catch anything. At daybreak, Jesus called to them from the shore. He told them to cast their nets on the right side of the boat. They doubted they'd catch anything. But again, they decided to do what Jesus asked. They caught 153 fish.

At that time in history, there were 153 nations. Jesus rewarded Peter's first catch by making him His disciple. The second catch was how Jesus released His disciples to preach the gospel to every nation. God wants you to trust Him and His will for your life. He wants you to try what He asks you to do.

Let's Talk About It

What might Jesus want you to do as His disciple today?

Did You Know?

153 fish were caught, which symbolized the 153 nations that existed at that time.

16 The Storm

Jesus deliberately chose the northern shore on the Sea of Galilee as the base for His teaching ministry. On the surrounding hillsides and along the shore, He taught the crowds.

That's one reason Jesus used so many fishing comparisons. They helped the people in this area understand His message.

The Sea of Galilee was important to the Jewish people. They fished on it and traveled by boat over it. But the Sea had a darker side, and the Jewish people knew it.

Cool winds blew off the mountains to the east. Then this air quickly sank. It displaced the warmer air on the surface of the water. This mixing of hot and cold produced severe storms.

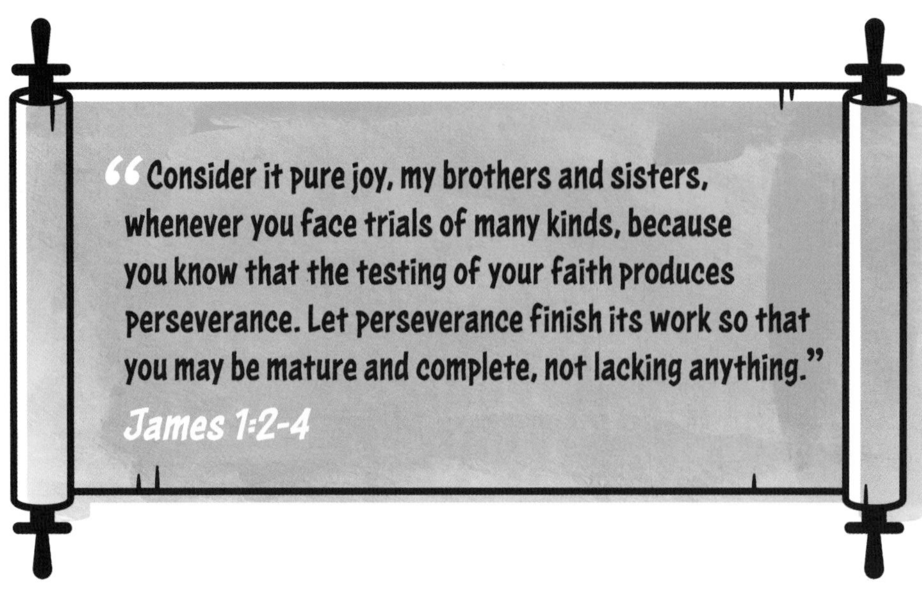

Jesus and His disciples were caught in a number of violent storms. Through them, Jesus taught His disciples many lessons. God wants you to understand the same lessons Jesus taught His disciples: You can count on God's help. He is bigger than any storm.

What are your storms? Sometimes your struggles may feel like a violent storm. They are frightening, chaotic, and confusing. During these difficult times, God wants you to trust Him. He wants you to tell Him when things are hard.

Sometimes God will answer your prayers exactly as you want. Sometimes He'll answer them in a different way. And sometimes you'll keep looking for His answers but won't see them. Only years later, as you look back over your life, will you see how He truly did answer your prayers. Some answers take longer or have a longer answer than others. Regardless, when you face storms in your life, you can count on God to help you.

Let's Talk About It

How can unfairness, mean kids, or even difficult tasks be a storm?

What is a storm in your life?

Have you asked God to help you with it?

Did You Know?

The sides of the boat were low.

Did You Know?

Their boat was probably only 26 feet long and 7 ½ feet wide.

17

Peter Walks on Water

Although the Sea of Galilee is called a sea, it's really a freshwater lake. The Jordan River flows into it from the north. This deep, blue body of water is more than twelve miles long and eight miles at its widest.

One day Jesus' disciples left the city of Capernaum by boat. After they were far from the shore, a squall suddenly came upon them. They strained at the oars to reach safety, but they made little progress. The waves crashed against their boat, and there was nothing they could do.

In the middle of the gale, one of the disciples saw Jesus. He wasn't in a boat. He was walking toward them on the violent swells of the waves.

> "'Lord, if it's you,' Peter replied, 'tell me to come to you on the water.' 'Come,' he said. Then Peter got down out of the boat, walked on the water and came toward Jesus. But when he saw the wind, he was afraid and, beginning to sink, cried out, 'Lord, save me!' Immediately Jesus reached out his hand and caught him. 'You of little faith,' he said, 'why did you doubt?'"
>
> *Matthew 14:28-31*

Peter wanted to be like Jesus. So when Jesus told him to step out of the boat and come to Him, Peter didn't hesitate. What went through Peter's mind? At first, he may have thought about reaching Jesus. But the waves started to crash against his body, and the winds howled around him. He grew scared and started to sink. Peter cried out to Jesus for help, and Jesus grabbed Peter's hand and pulled him to safety.

Peter didn't do everything right. But he did step out of the boat to follow Jesus. Peter had the faith to trust Jesus and do what Jesus wanted him to do.

You can be like Peter, even when you mess up. Trust God without hesitation, and do what He says in His Word. Perhaps someday you'll also walk on water.

Let's Talk About It

In what area do you need Peter's faith to follow Jesus?

How can you keep your eyes on Jesus and not on the squall?

Did You Know?

The Sea of Galilee is more than 150 feet deep.

Did You Know?

The Sea of Galilee is the largest body of fresh water in Israel.

18 Jesus Feeds the Multitudes

Have you ever heard it said that Jesus is "the Bread of Life"? Jesus used these exact words in the Bible to describe Himself. He said that anyone who comes to Him will never be hungry, and that everyone who believes in Him will never be thirsty.

> "Then Jesus directed them to have all the people sit down in groups on the green grass. So they sat down in groups of hundreds and fifties. Taking the five loaves and the two fish and looking up to heaven, he gave thanks and broke the loaves. Then he gave them to his disciples to distribute to the people. He also divided the two fish among them all. They all ate and were satisfied, and the disciples picked up twelve basketfuls of broken pieces of bread and fish."
>
> *Mark 6:39-43*

As Jesus traveled across the land, large crowds would gather to hear Him speak. One time Jesus and His disciples tried to get away from the crowds by sailing to a remote location where they could rest. But lots of people recognized the group and ran after them on foot.

When Jesus got off the boat, a big crowd was already gathered near the shore. Jesus felt compassion for the large group, so He began to teach them. But when evening came, the disciples wanted to send the people away so they could find food to eat. Instead, Jesus took the only food they had—five loaves of bread and two fish—said a blessing, and handed out the food. Even though there were 5,000 men in the crowd (and probably thousands more women and children), there were still twelve baskets' worth of leftovers after everyone had eaten.

How can someone feed thousands of people with just five loaves and two fish? It was a miracle! And you know what else? Jesus did the same thing a short time later when He fed 4,000 men with seven loaves of bread and a few small fish. This time, there were seven baskets of leftover food.

Do you know what it feels like to be hungry? Of course you do. God made our bodies so that we can't live for a long time without food. People need bread (food) in order to live, but Jesus is the "bread" we need for eternal life—life with Him in heaven. If you ask Him, God will give you the spiritual food you need. After all, God already gave us His Son, the Bread of Life.

Let's Talk About It

Have you trusted in Jesus to be your own Bread of Life?

How does Jesus feed us spiritually day by day?

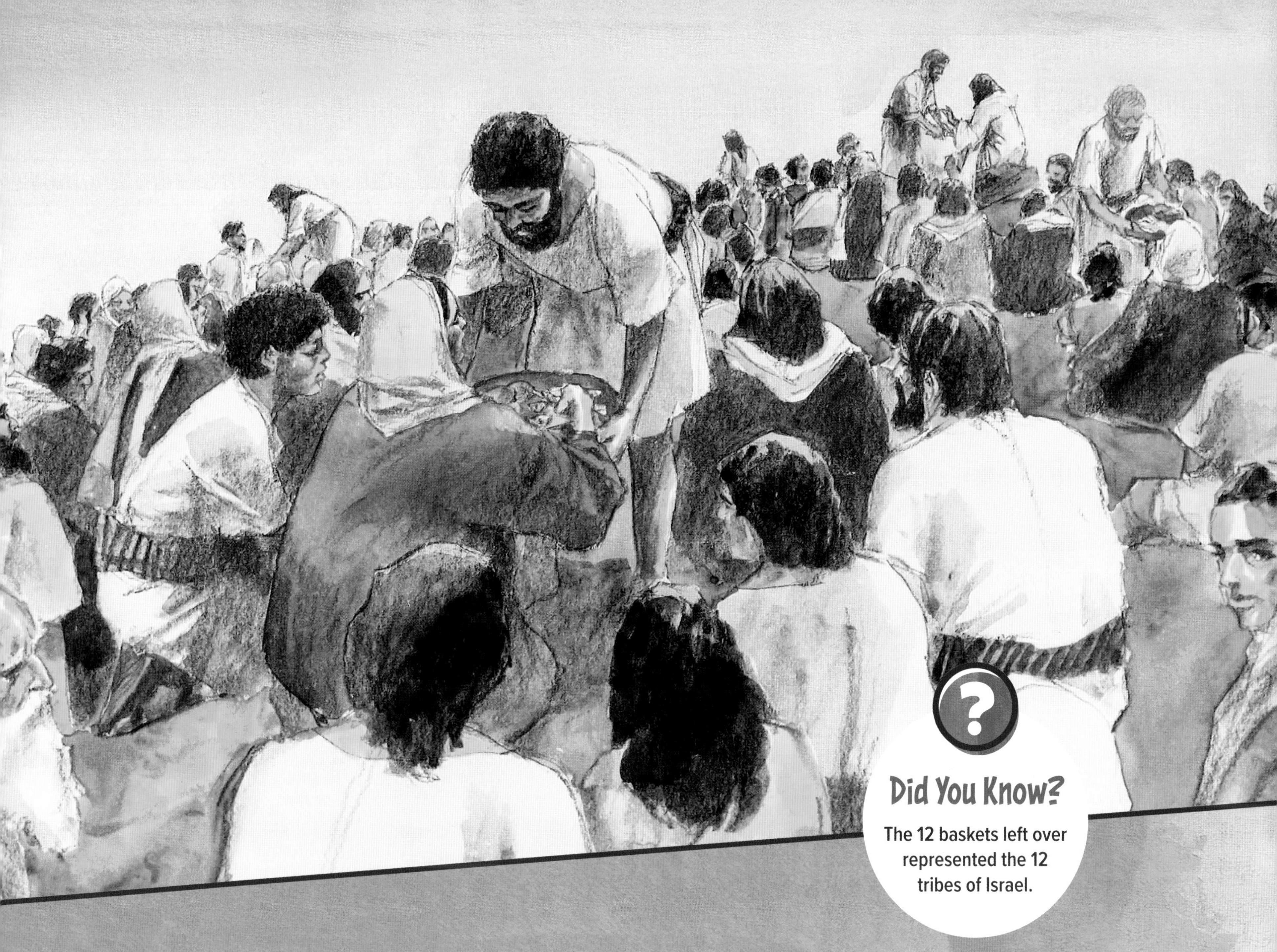

Did You Know?

The 12 baskets left over represented the 12 tribes of Israel.

19 Healing of the Demon-Possessed Man

Jesus used lots of different ways to describe Himself. In John 8, He said, "I am the light of the world." And what does light do? Well, for one thing, it chases away darkness.

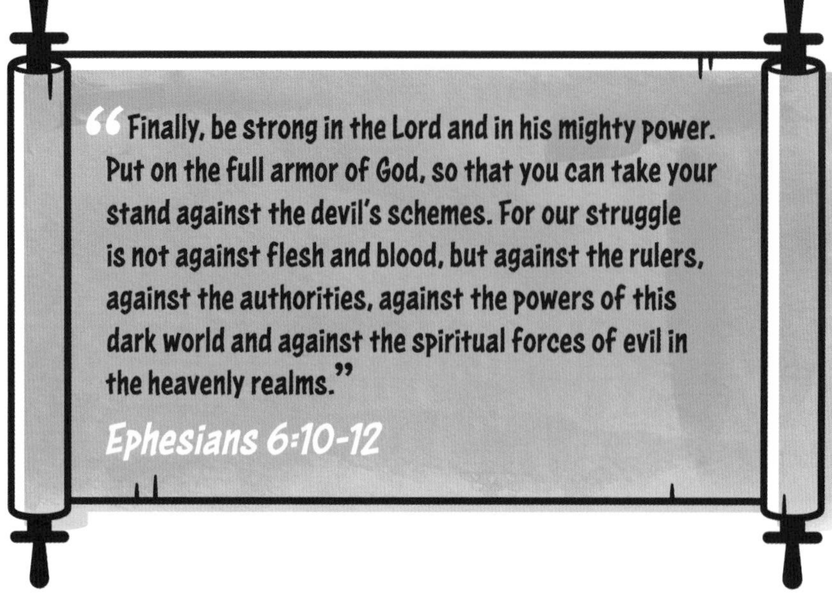

Wherever He went, Jesus—the Light of the World—always stood up to spiritual darkness. When Jesus and His disciples sailed across the Sea of Galilee, they met a man on the shore who was possessed (controlled) by evil spirits. Jesus healed the man and broke Satan's power by sending the evil spirits out of the man and into a nearby herd of pigs. The entire herd of about 2,000 pigs ran into the sea and drowned.

This use of Jesus' power had such a strong impact on the local people that they begged Jesus to leave their land. The man Jesus healed wanted to go with Him, but Jesus had something else in mind. Jesus told the man to tell others in the land what God had done for him.

The man told his friends and others how Jesus had healed him—how the light of God had defeated spiritual darkness. The Bible says the people were amazed by what had happened.

Are there people and places that seem dark and evil to you—so dark that you try to avoid them? God says He will protect us from evil, and He gives us His armor to wear. But God's armor isn't made of metal like the armor knights wore. Ephesians 6 says that faith in God is our shield, and the Word of God (the Bible) is our sword. When we put on the whole armor of God, we are better prepared for spiritual battles against darkness. When you feel afraid of evil or darkness, pray and ask God for courage, and for opportunities to help others. If you're not sure where to begin, just telling people about how God has helped you is a great way to let His light shine in the darkness.

Let's Talk About It

How can you be a light for God in a dark world?

Did You Know?

Pigs were considered sacred in this area.

20 A Living God

Imagine following Jesus for two days over rough hills and rocky ground to a land where the people built temples to false gods. And when they arrived, Jesus asked them an important question: "Who do you think I am?"

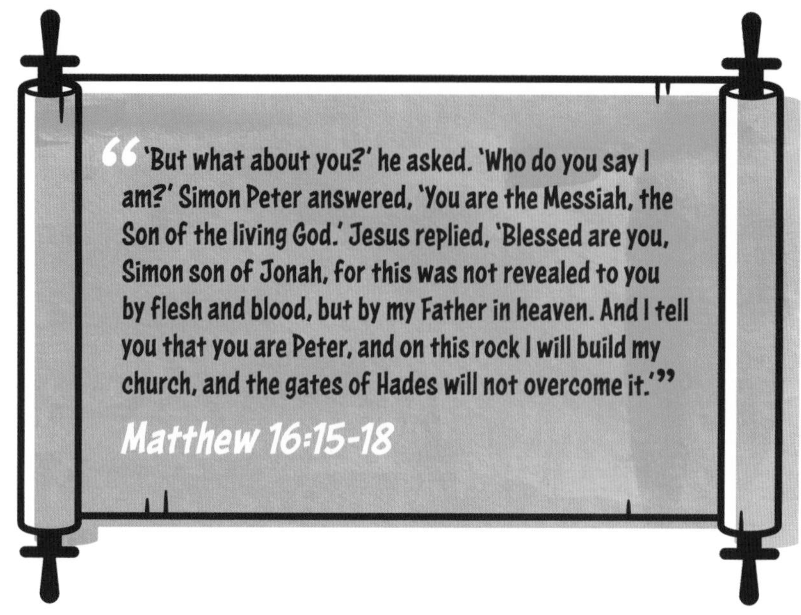

Peter, one of Jesus' disciples, replied, "You are the Christ, the Son of the Living God."

Peter got it! Jesus was pleased with this answer, because Peter understood that Jesus was the Son of God—the one true Savior of the world. Because they worshipped statues and other false gods, the people of this land were really serving Satan (the devil). But Jesus told Peter that He would build a church that could overcome all the power and strength of the devil!

Jesus also said "the gates of hell" would not be stronger than His church. People build gates to keep out their enemies. But Jesus was saying that if His church followed Him faithfully, it could defeat even the gates of hell. Jesus Himself defeated death when He rose from the grave after He was crucified. Because of who He is and how He suffered, anyone who believes in Jesus will receive eternal life with Him.

Jesus spent three years teaching His disciples and preparing them for life after He was gone. In the same way, it is our job as followers of Jesus to help build His church and to overcome the gates of hell. But we can't do it alone. We need to rely on Jesus' strength and power.

The best way to do this is to trust in the true, living God, and not the dead "gods" that some people serve. What are some of the false idols people worship today—things like riches, beauty, possessions, or being famous? What are some false gods that can sometimes distract you from serving the one true God? Pray and ask God to help you serve only Him.

Let's Talk About It

What would you say if someone asked you who Jesus is?

Did You Know?

Caesarea Philippi is the site of a great pagan temple dedicated to Pan, the Roman fertility god.

21 The Temple

Jesus was in Jerusalem, at the Temple. The Temple was the center of religious life for the Jewish people. It was where God dwelled among them. Through the prophet Isaiah many years before, God had said He wanted all people who believed in Him to come here and worship (see Isaiah 56:6-7).

But the people who ran the Temple had turned it into a business. They made others who wanted to make a sacrifice for their sins buy the animals from them. And people could only buy the animals with Temple money, so they first had to trade the money they had in their pockets for the Temple money. The Temple leaders made the people pay a fee for that trade, too.

Jesus was upset when He saw all this buying and selling and money-changing going on. The Temple was supposed to be a place for worship and prayer. He was also upset that the Temple leaders were making it so hard for the people to worship. So He took action and drove out all those sellers and buyers and moneychangers.

Today, God still wants all believers from every part of the world to worship Him freely. But we do not have to go to just one place, like the Temple, to do that. We can worship Him in our churches or even in our own homes. We know He sees us and hears us wherever we are.

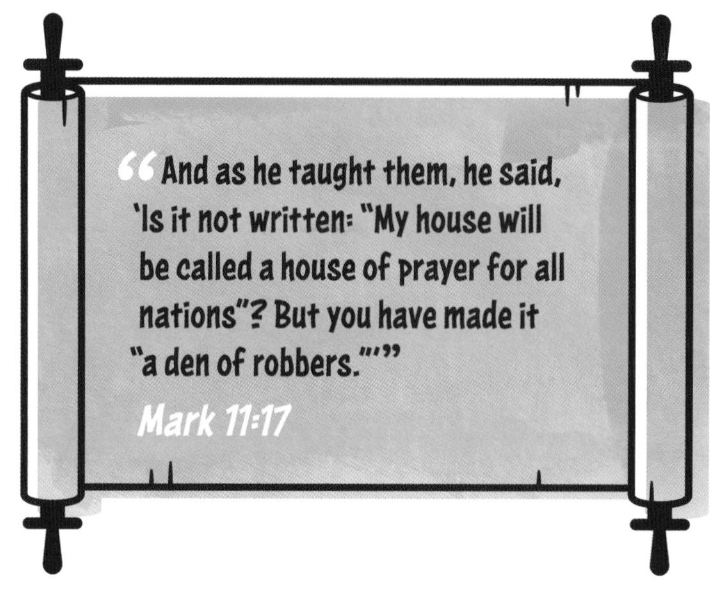

Let's Talk About It

What are some of the ways we can worship God today?

What's your favorite way to worship Him?

Did You Know?

The Temple was made of marble and gold and was taller than a 15-story building.

Did You Know?

There were 8 different courts within the Temple.

22 Jesus the Scapegoat

The religious leaders of Jesus' day were angry with Him. They stirred up the people to make Pontius Pilate, the Roman ruler over them, condemn Jesus to death on a cross. What they did not see, however, was that in doing this terrible thing, they were fulfilling God's plan to offer salvation to all people who put their trust in Jesus.

Jesus lived a perfect life. He never sinned, never said or did anything selfish or mean. He never cheated anyone or told lies about others. He is the only person who ever lived a sinless life. So when He died on the cross, He did not need to pay a penalty for sins of His own. Instead, He, the Son of God, paid the penalty for our sins.

> "The high priest carries the blood of animals into the Most Holy Place as a sin offering, but the bodies are burned outside the camp. And so Jesus also suffered outside the city gate to make the people holy through his own blood."
>
> *Hebrews 13:11-12*

In Old Testament times, on the Day of Atonement, God had the high priest put his hands on the head of a live goat and confess the sins of the Israelite people. Then this scapegoat, symbolically carrying the sins of all the people, was led outside the camp. At a remote place in the desert, the goat was released. (See Leviticus 16.)

In a similar way, when Jesus was going to be crucified, He was taken outside the city gates to a place called Golgotha. Like the scapegoat, He carried away the guilt for our sins. But He carried the sins of all people, not just the Israelites. And He removed our guilt for all time. Those wrong things we have thought, said, and done no longer stand between God and us if we have trusted in Jesus to be our Savior.

Let's Talk About It

Have you trusted in Jesus to be your Savior?

If not, would you like to do that today?

Did You Know?

The route to go outside the city would have been very busy, loud, and smelly.

Did You Know?

It was a very public place for an execution.

23 The Lamb of God

In the Bible, Jesus is often called the Lamb of God. For instance, when John the Baptist saw Jesus coming one day, he (John) said, "Look, the Lamb of God, who takes away the sin of the world" (John 1:29).

That title refers to the time when the Israelite people were slaves in Egypt. To force the Egyptian pharaoh (king) to free them, God sent ten plagues on the land. The last of those was the death of the firstborn in all Egyptian households. The Israelite people showed their trust in God by doing what He asked. Each family sacrificed a lamb and put its blood on the doorposts of their home right before that terrible night.

> "For you know that it was not with perishable things such as silver or gold that you were redeemed from the empty way of life handed down to you from your ancestors, but with the precious blood of Christ, a lamb without blemish or defect. He was chosen before the creation of the world, but was revealed in these last times for your sake. Through him you believe in God, who raised him from the dead and glorified him, and so your faith and hope are in God."
>
> *1 Peter 1:18-21*

When the angel of God saw that blood on a home's doorway, he "passed over" those homes and left everyone alive inside. And ever since that night, the Jewish people have celebrated Passover every year to remember that event.

We call the day Jesus made His big entry into Jerusalem Palm Sunday. And in God's perfect plan, it was the very day the Jews were selecting the lambs to be sacrificed on Passover. Jesus was saying clearly, "I am the perfect lamb, the perfect sacrifice. I will die for the sins of all people—just as John the Baptist said."

Let's Talk About It

Jesus sacrificed Himself to pay the penalty for the bad things we've thought, said, and done. How does that make you feel about Him?

Did You Know?

The lambs had to be pure and spotless.

24 Jesus Cries

In Luke 19:41-44, the Bible tells us that as Jesus entered Jerusalem on Palm Sunday, He cried. Why? Because the people didn't understand His purpose and plan. And they would suffer as a result.

The people thought their Messiah would be a king who would free them from Roman rule. Even Jesus' closest followers thought He was going to be that kind of savior. But Jesus did not come to be an earthly king. He was not a political leader. He came for a far more important purpose. He came to serve, not to be served like a king. And His ultimate act of service would be to pay the price for our sins by dying on the cross in our place just a week later.

Earlier, Jesus had shown His disciples how to serve in simple ways by washing their dirty feet. When He was done, He told them, "Now that I, your Lord and Teacher, have washed your feet, you also should wash one another's feet. I have set you an example that you should do as I have done for you." (John 13:14-15).

Today we are Jesus' disciples if we trust in Him as our Savior. So He wants us, too, to follow His example and serve others every day.

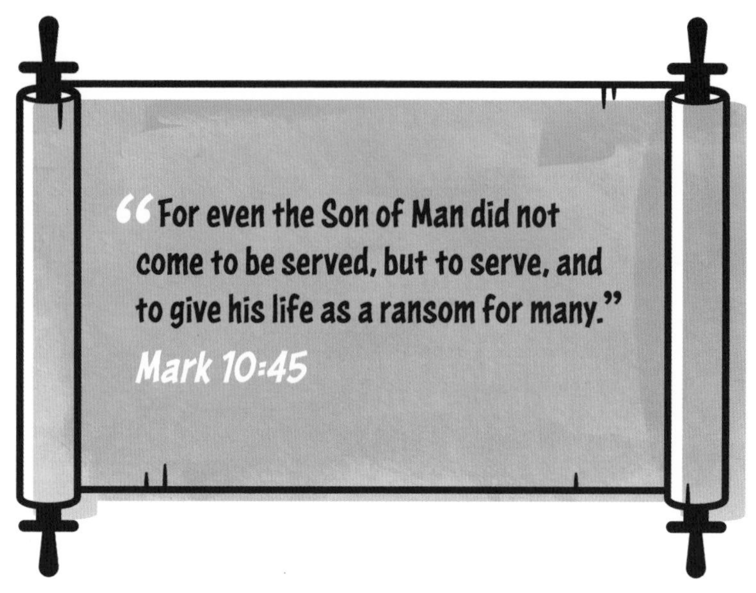

Let's Talk About It

What are some ways you could serve a family member or a friend today?

Did You Know?

Hosanna means "deliver me."

25 The Olive Tree

An olive tree grows olives, right? And some olives are used to make olive oil, which many people today use for cooking. The growing of olives and the making of olive oil were very important businesses in Jesus' time on earth, too.

During the three years of His public ministry, Jesus lived and spent much of His time in an area called Capernaum. People grew a lot of olives and made a lot of olive oil there. And to get the oil from the olives, they would crush and press them under large, heavy stones.

On Jesus' last night before His crucifixion, He went to the Garden of Gethsemane. That means "Garden of the Olive Press," so it was in or near a grove of olive trees on the Mount of Olives. (That's a lot of olives!)

Jesus knew He was going to be arrested that night. He also knew He would be whipped and then killed the next day. So, as the saying goes, He felt a lot of weight on His shoulders that night in the garden. The weight of abandonment and denial by His disciples. Of an unfair trial. Of the torture of a Roman whip. Of the pain of crucifixion and death. And, worst of all, the turning away of God the Father when He (Jesus) took the sins of the world upon Himself.

Jesus was in the place of all those olives. And the weights used to process them were symbols of all the weight He felt that night. He felt so much pressure that the Bible says He was in agony and "his sweat became like great drops of blood." But He willingly went through all of that for you and me. He took upon Himself the pain and the penalty we deserved. *That's how much He loves us.*

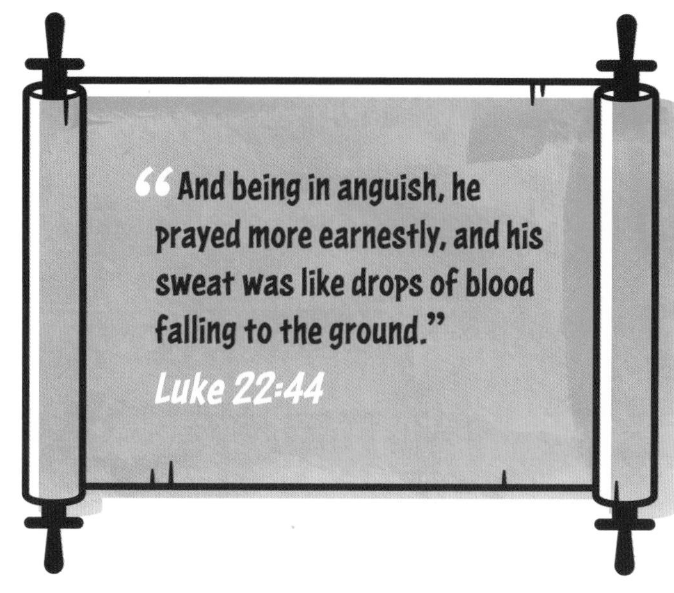

Let's Talk About It

What can you do today to show Jesus how much you love *Him*?

Did You Know?

An olive crusher was a large, round stone basin.

Did You Know?

Gethsemane means “a place for pressing oil.”

26 To Become Like a Child

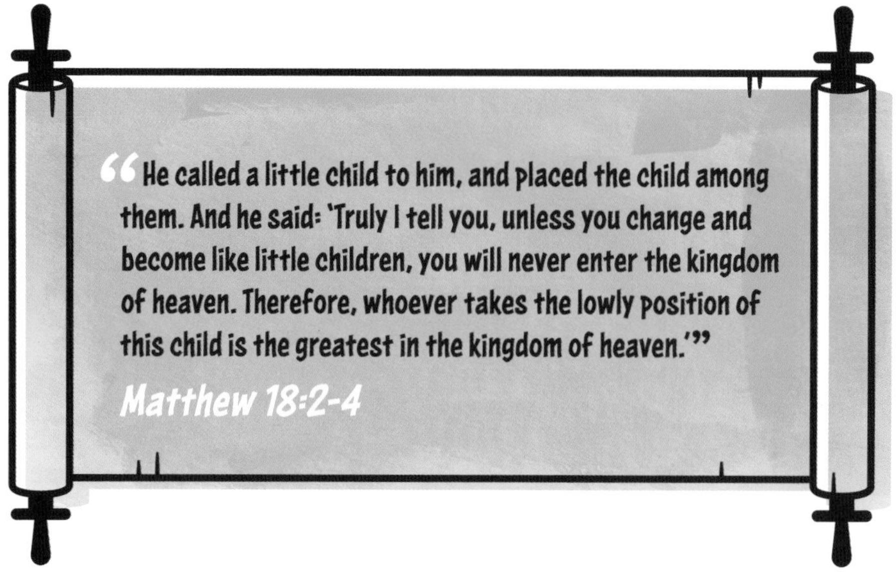

“He called a little child to him, and placed the child among them. And he said: ‘Truly I tell you, unless you change and become like little children, you will never enter the kingdom of heaven. Therefore, whoever takes the lowly position of this child is the greatest in the kingdom of heaven.’”

Matthew 18:2-4

Jesus’ disciples thought He would soon set up an earthly kingdom. And they were so proud that they thought they should have special places of honor there. They even asked Him who would be the greatest. They felt it should be one of them.

The first part of Jesus’ answer is in the Bible quote above. To understand it, you need to know that back in those days, children weren’t valued very highly. They didn’t have much status. They would have been considered among the *least important* people in society.

Because of that, most children would have been humble in the presence of adults. They probably stood at the back of the crowd surrounding Jesus and His disciples. The adults likely thought of them as just getting in the way.

That’s why Jesus told His disciples they needed to turn—away from their pride—and become like children—humble and even unimportant in the world’s eyes. *Then* they would be great in the kingdom of *heaven*—the kingdom that’s far more valuable and important than any earthly land.

We have great worth in God’s eyes. He loves us so much! But like the disciples, we too should have a humble view of ourselves. As the apostle Paul wrote in the Bible, “Don’t do anything only to get ahead. Don’t do it because you are proud. Instead, be humble. Value others more than yourselves. None of you should look out just for your own good. Each of you should also look out for the good of others” (Philippians 2:3-4, NIrV).

Let’s Talk About It

Knowing God loves us should help us to serve and care for *others*. How could you put someone else’s good ahead of your own today?

Did You Know?

Children were considered unimportant during that time.

27 Jesus' Death

In the days when Jesus was on earth, the priests (who were supposed to care for the people spiritually) would sacrifice a lamb. The lamb had to be pure white, without any spots or marks. When the priest would kill the lamb, it was a symbol to God that the people were sorry for their sins and wanted His forgiveness.

The blood of the lamb proved they were sincere. The problem was, the blood of the little lamb couldn't take away the sins of the people.

The same is true for us today. The blood of an animal can't take away our sins and mistakes. There's only one thing that can, and that is the blood of Jesus. That's why He had to die on the cross for us.

But even harder than dying on the cross was being separated from His Father for the first time in all of history. He cried out from the cross, "Eli, Eli, lema sabachthani?" It means, "My God, my God, why have you forsaken me?" Can you imagine being separated from the person who loves you the most? It would be very frightening and sad.

Jesus had to experience that pain so we could be forgiven of our sins. Just like the lambs, He died for us. But unlike the lamb's blood, the blood of Jesus lasts forever. Because He died for us, we don't ever have to worry about being apart from God. Jesus made sure that we can be with God forever if we will trust Him for forgiveness.

What an amazing gift!

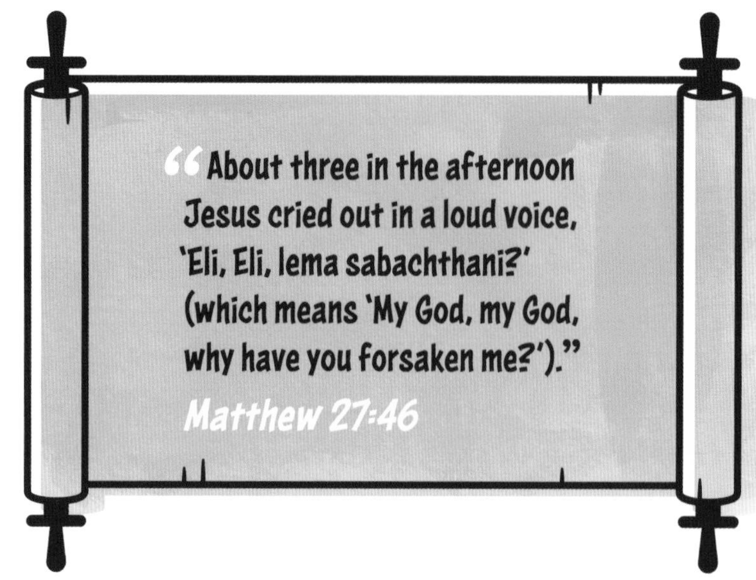

Let's Talk About It

Take a moment to think about how much Jesus suffered for you. Then thank Him for going through all that to take away your sins forever.

Did You Know?

Jesus died at 3:00 p.m., the same time the priest would kill a lamb for the sins of the whole nation.

28 Jesus' Burial and Resurrection

People don't come back from the dead—at least, not most people. On the third day after Jesus was crucified, the disciples—and everyone else—thought He was dead in the tomb.

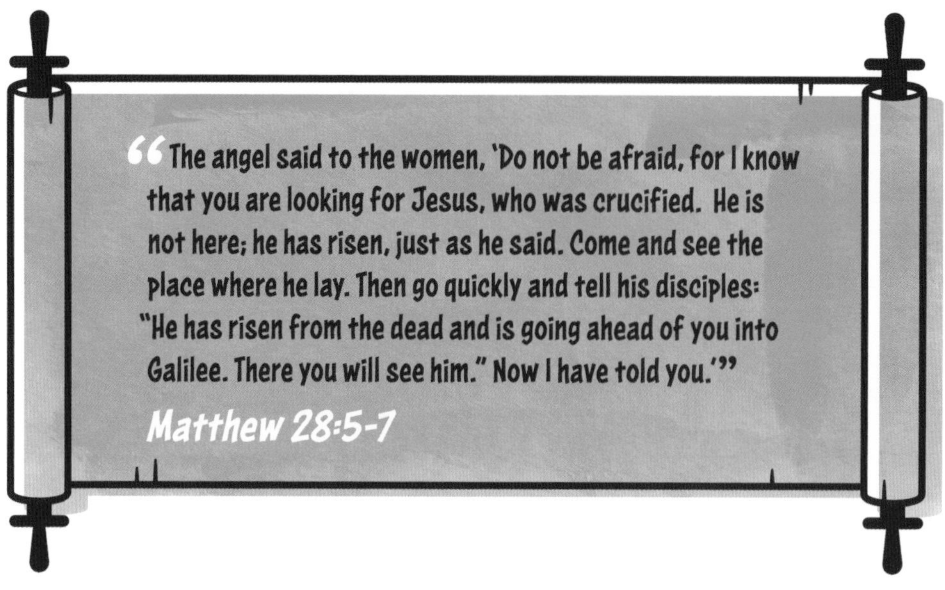

No one thought they would ever see Him again. That made His followers very sad. It made His enemies very happy. But His followers and His enemies were in for a big surprise.

The Bible tells us two ladies named Mary went to see the body of Jesus. But when they got there, an angel was waiting to tell them news that was so good, they could hardly believe it. Jesus was alive. He had risen from the dead!

It's hard to believe someone could die and then come back to life, but Jesus did. What's even better, He's still alive today, and one day those who trust in Him will live with Him forever in heaven.

The fact that Jesus is alive is the best news we could ever receive. But we have to believe it's true. Sometimes that's difficult. But when we trust in Him, He fills our hearts and promises He will be with us every day of our lives.

Let's Talk About It

Jesus is alive! Talk about how important it is, not just that Jesus died for your sins, but also that He rose from the dead so you could be with Him forever.

Did You Know?
A tomb cost a year's salary.
Did You Know?
The tomb was cut from rock and sealed with a large stone.

29 The Price of a Bride

In ancient times, when a young man wanted to marry a young woman, he would meet with her parents and offer a gift for the privilege of making their daughter his wife. Can you imagine having to make a deal to marry someone?

You would really have to love that person if you were willing to pay a high price. But that's exactly what Jesus did when He died for us on the cross. He loved us so much that He was willing to pay with His blood so we could have an eternal relationship with Him. The Bible tells us His followers are actually called "the Bride of Christ."

> "The Lord Jesus, on the night he was betrayed, took bread, and when he had given thanks, he broke it and said, 'This is my body, which is for you; do this in remembrance of me.' In the same way, after supper he took the cup, saying, 'This cup is the new covenant in my blood; do this, whenever you drink it, in remembrance of me.' For whenever you eat this bread and drink this cup, you proclaim the Lord's death until he comes."
>
> *1 Corinthians 11:23-26*

When a couple gets married, they make a covenant with each other and God. A covenant is a promise you should never break. The amazing thing about God's covenant with us is that He will never break it because it cost Him so much to make it.

Jesus gave us a reminder of just how much He paid to make us His "bride." Often when we go to church, we share in Communion. That's where we take the bread that reminds us of His body, and we drink wine or juice from a cup that reminds us of the blood that flowed from His veins. The bread and the cup are reminders of just how much we are loved by God. He paid the ultimate price so we could be with Him forever. How cool is that!

Let's Talk About It

How much would you be willing to do for someone you love?

As you answer that question, thank God for how much He was willing to pay for a relationship with you.

Did You Know?

The marriage cup symbolized the Passover cup.

30 Power to the People

If you were a superhero, what would be your special power? It would be awesome to be able to fly, to have the strength to stop a train, or even to turn yourself invisible. We all want to be smart, strong, or special in some way. The fact is, God has made you special and has given you special abilities and powers you may not even know you have.

Jesus promised that when He left earth, He was going to send His Holy Spirit to live within us and give us power to live the way God wants us to.

So what does God want us to do with the power He gives us? First, He wants us to tell others about everything He's done for us. He also wants us to love each other in special ways, like being kind, patient, and humble. These things can be hard to do at times, but God's Spirit gives us the power we need to serve Him and others.

You may not feel like a comic book superhero, but you're even better. You have the power of God inside you to do special things. Imagine the difference you can make by encouraging someone who feels down or left out. Imagine the joy you can give by feeding someone who is hungry or by giving a coat to someone who is cold.

And the best part is, you don't need to fly or lift heavy stuff! You just need to trust God for the power He's given you to do even better things.

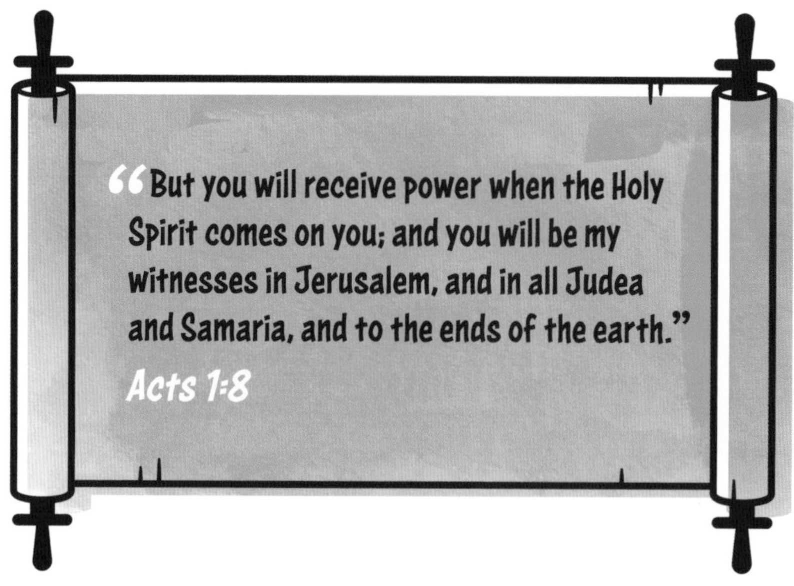

Let's Talk About It

What special powers do you think God has given you?

How can you use them to help others see His love?

Did You Know?

The Holy Spirit came to live in Jesus' disciples 10 days after Jesus ascended into heaven.

As an NFL quarterback, I know a lot about being dirty and sweaty. But years ago, when I was privileged to have Ray Vander Laan as my high school Bible teacher, he shared a beautiful thought that has stuck with me to this day. He reminded me that the disciples often walked so closely with Jesus that the dust from His sandals would kick up on their feet. He used this as an analogy to challenge me to be so close to the Messiah that I would be covered in His presence. I've never forgotten that lesson. As you share these devotions with your children and family, I pray that you sense the closeness of Jesus in new and profound ways.

—Kirk Cousins
NFL QUARTERBACK